Secrets of Lemon Rediscovered

ADISH Books

ISBN-10: 1491285109
ISBN-13: 978-1491285107

Disclaimer

The information specified throughout this book is provided for general information only, and should not be treated as a substitute for the medical advice of your own doctor, psychiatrist, medical counselor or any other health care professional. Nothing contained on this book is intended to be for medical diagnosis or treatment. By following the instructions contained herein, the reader willingly assumes all risks in connection with such instructions. If you think you have a medical emergency, call your doctor immediately.

Lemon and Lemon Essential Oil: History, Varieties and Uses

The lemon fruit is a hybrid of sour orange and citron. It grows on a small evergreen tree that is native to Asia, but is cultivated throughout many parts of the world. Lemons are primarily used for their juice, which is about 5% citric acid with a sour taste. The rinds of lemons are also used for culinary purposes.

Although the exact origin of the lemon tree is unknown, it likely first grew in China, Burma and Southern India. Lemon trees were introduced to Europe around the 1st century AD, then to Persia, Egypt and Iraq around 700 AD. By 1150 AD, lemons were widely cultivated in the Mediterranean region and used in Islamic gardens throughout the Arab world.

Christopher Columbus brought lemon seeds to the Americas in 1493. Spanish conquests in the New World then spread the seeds, where the plants were used for medicinal purposes. In the 1800's, lemon trees were widely planted in California and Florida.

Today, there are many varieties of the lemon tree. The Eureka is the lemon most commonly found in supermarkets. This variety is popular because of the plant's ability to produce fruit throughout the year, giving it the nickname "four seasons". The fruit of the Lisbon tree is similar to that of the Eureka with high, acidic juice levels. The Femminello St. Teresa, also known as the Sorrento or Sfusato, is grown in Italy and used in the making of lemoncello.

The Meyer lemon was discovered by Frank N. Meyer in 1908. Because of the Meyer's thin skin and rind, extra care is needed to ship this variety of lemon. For this reason, they are not widely commercially grown. However, the Meyer lemon is more frost tolerant and less acidic than other lemon varieties.

Lemons have many uses, as follows -

-Detoxification
-Culinary purpose
-Food preservative
-Aromatherapy
-Cleaning agent
-Deodorize
-Disinfect
-Skin cleanser

Lemonade, cocktails and many soft drinks are made with lemon juice. Lemon juice is often used to marinade fish. The acid in the juice neutralizes harmful amines and converts them to ammonium salts.

Lemon juice can be used as a preservative on fruits and vegetables like apples and avocados to prevent oxidation and browning after the foods are sliced. Preserved lemons like lemon pickle are also a common part of Moroccan and Indian cuisine.

Lemon zest is made by scraping away little pieces from the colorful outer layer of the skin of a lemon. It is then used to add flavor to foods. The zest of a lemon contains essential oil with a strong, delicious flavor. It can be added to cakes, cookies, risottos and lots of other recipes to add a little extra zing.

Lemon juice also has many uses as a cleaning agent. It can be used to deodorize, disinfect, remove stains and grease and act as a non toxic insecticide. The lemon peel is often used as a wood cleaner and polish.

Lemon oil is obtained from lemon zest and used in aromatherapy to enhance mood. It is also used in Indian medical practices like Ayurveda and Siddha Medicine. As an essential oil, lemon oil has a wide variety of uses, from a skin cleanser to a natural fragrance.

How to Store Lemons, Lemon Juice and Lemon Zest

Lemons can be left out at room temperature for a week. However, they will begin to dry out during this time. If

you are not planning on using your
lemons within a few days of purchase,
store them in the refrigerator to
maintain freshness. To keep your
lemons away from damaging moisture,
place them in a ziplock bag and squeeze
out the air. When lemons are in an
airtight plastic bag and placed in the
refrigerator, they will remain fresh for
up to a month.

Lemon juice can be stored in the
refrigerator for about four days. Make
sure that you strain out the seeds, as
they will cause the lemon juice to
become bitter. To store lemon juice for
longer amounts of time, it can be frozen.
One easy method is to make lemon juice
ice cubes using an ice tray. Once frozen,
the lemon ice cubes can be stored in a
ziplock bag in the freezer for several
months.

You can also store lemon juice for long amounts of time by canning it. Use a glass container approved for canning purposes. Fill the jar leaving a 1/4 inch gap between the juice and rim of the can. Screw the lid on tightly. Then, place the can in a large stockpot covered by about two inches of water and the stockpot lid. If you are using a pint or quart sized jar, boil the water for five minutes. If using a half-gallon jar, boil for 10 minutes. After boiling, when the jar is cool, press on the lid. If it does not pop, the jar is properly sealed.

To preserve lemon zest, store it in the freezer in an airtight freezer bag. The zest will lose a little bit of flavor but will still add delicious taste to your recipes. Adding a few tablespoons of lemon juice to the freezer bag may help hold in moisture and flavor.

Safety with Pure Lemon Essential Oil

Lemons, lemon juice and lemon essential oil is non-toxic. It can generally be used internally and externally safely. However, lemon juice or oil may cause skin irritation or allergic reaction in some individuals. To prevent a serious reaction, test lemon products on a small area of the skin. If no adverse effects occur, use freely.

Lemons, their juice and lemon oil are phototoxic. This means that when exposed to sunlight, a chemical reaction can cause skin irritation similar to a sunburn. Do not use lemon products either internally or externally prior to sun exposure.

Health Benefits of Lemon and Lemon Essential Oil

Lemon and its oil is used all over the world for natural healing and wellness. It possesses antiseptic, antibacterial, antiviral and antifungal properties.

Detoxification

Lemon is known as a fantastic detoxifier. It can increase circulation and promote the elimination of toxins from the body. Many people use lemon daily, or for a set period of time, such as during a cleanse, to rid the blood, liver and other organs of harmful pollutants.

Weight Loss

Essential lemon oil, lemons and lemon juice can be used in several ways to help promote weight loss. When ingested, lemon products will boost the metabolism and help rid the body of harmful fat cells. When applied directly to the skin, lemon oil will fight cellulite and promote fat burning. The pleasing scent of lemons may also help to promote a feeling of fullness, prevent emotional eating and curb hunger and cravings.

Clinical studies have proven that lemon lowers and helps to normalize blood sugar levels almost immediately upon exposure. Apply a few drops of oil to your wrists or the bottom of your feet to naturally and effectively lower blood sugar levels.

Diabetes

Lemon oil can also benefit those with diabetes by improving circulation. Many diabetics suffer from poor circulation which can lead to stroke, blood clots, heart attack and many other dangerous conditions. Adding a drop of lemon oil to each glass of water drunk throughout the day will help diabetics maintain healthy veins and arteries.

Osteoporosis

Those with osteoporosis or other bone-related conditions can benefit from ingesting lemon juice daily. Acid causes the body to take calcium from the bones, causing bone weakness. Eating alkaline foods, like lemons, prevents excess acid and protects the bones. Drinking a cup of hot water with lemon juice daily can protect the bones from calcium loss and weakness. A bit of cayenne pepper can be added for even more alkaline benefits.

Insomnia

Lemon juice can be used by insomniacs to help them achieve a peaceful, restful night of sleep. The sour, tangy smell of lemon juice has a calming effect. A cup of warm juice with a bit of honey before bed is known to go a long way to help put you to sleep.

Immunity Boosting

Ingesting lemons and lemon juice can boost your immunity. Lemons are full of potassium and vitamin C which will help power the immune system and fight off colds and the flu.

Cough and Cold

Lemon juice and honey can be used to help soothe the symptoms of cough and cold. The lemon juice breaks up mucus while the honey coats the throat, relieving sore throat and suppressing cough. Add lemon juice and a tablespoon of honey to a cup of warm water to try this easy, natural remedy the next time you have a bothersome cold!

Travel Sickness

Travel sickness, nausea and vomiting can be treated with lemon. To get rid of any kind of nausea or upset stomach, suck on a lemon wedge for a few minutes or until symptoms subside. Alternatively, you can drink the juice. Be sure to rinse your mouth out or brush your teeth after ingesting lemon juice as the acids present can cause damage to tooth enamel.

The fresh, tangy scent of lemons can brighten the mood and soothe symptoms of anxiety. Next time you're feeling stressed or overwhelmed, drink a glass of warm water and lemon juice. Or, simply cut up a lemon and let the refreshing scent fill the room. You can also use lemon oil to lift your mood. Try putting a few drops on your wrists and gently inhaling the scent at intervals throughout your day to maintain a positive mood.

Acne

Lemons contain hydroxy acid. This acid is commonly used in products designed to get rid of dead skin, unclog pores and eliminate acne and scarring. Instead of spending money on these expensive products, you can treat acne and acne scars using lemons. Juice a lemon and soak a cotton ball in the juice. Gently wipe the juice on your face and leave for several minutes before rinsing off. Some people are sensitive to this technique, so you might want to test a small area before applying lemon juice to your whole face. If burning, peeling or irritation occurs, discontinue use. To make the juice a little less potent and potentially irritating, you can dilute it with water.

Heartburn

You would think that the acidic properties of lemons would make them harmful to those suffering from heartburn or reflux disease. But, lemons can actually help some with these painful, irritating conditions. When a lemon or lemon juice is digested, it has an alkalizing effect on the body, which is the opposite of an acidifying effect. So, consuming lemons or lemon juice can actually help prevent symptoms of excessive acid. Try drinking a cup of warm water and lemon juice each morning to raise the pH level of your body. Although this treatment helps many people, there are exceptions and it is possible that consuming lemon juice could actually worsen your symptoms. So, proceed with caution and if this technique makes your heartburn worse, discontinue the practice.

Lemon Recipes for Personal Beauty Care

Just like cleaning solutions, beauty care products don't have to be expensive. By making your own products, you can save money, avoid harsh chemicals and use natural ingredients that are actually good for you.

Lemon and Yogurt Face Mask

Lemon and yogurt possess powerful ingredients that can contribute to beautiful, healthy skin. The lactic acid in yogurt helps remove dead skin and reduce the signs of aging. The zinc content will help clear acne, scarring and blemishes.

Ingredients:

-2 tablespoons plain, regular (not low fat) yogurt

-2 drops of lemon juice

-3 teaspoons honey

Procedure:

-Combine ingredients

-Apply to your face and leave on for 20-30 minutes

-Wash the mask off

Lemons contain alpha hydroxy acids that can also speed the disappearance of scars and increase skin elasticity. Use this mask to tighten, brighten and heal your skin.

Lemon Sugar Scrub

Use this simple scrub recipe to get refreshed and flawless smooth skin. The lemon will cleanse your skin and energize the senses while the sugar exfoliates, getting rid of dry, dead skin and leaving baby-softness in its place.

Ingredients:

-8 tablespoons lemon juice

-10-20 drops essential lemon oil

-2 cups olive oil

-5 1/8 cups sugar

Procedure:

-Mix ingredients in a large bowl

-Spoon or pour into desired containers

-Enjoy yourself or give as a gift

Lemon and Sea Salt Scrub

This scrub is perfect for softening the skin, getting rid of acne and scarring, and eliminating age spots. Sea salt and lemon are both antibacterial and work to cleanse and exfoliate. Using this scrub will give you brighter, softer and renewed skin.

Ingredients:

-1 lemon

-1 tablespoon olive oil

-5 tablespoons sea salt

Procedure:

-Thoroughly mix the olive oil and sea salt (if you don't mix these first, the lemon will dissolve the salt)

-Squeeze the lemon juice over the salt and oil

-Mix and enjoy!

Lemon Anti-wrinkle Toner

Use this toner to tighten and brighten the skin, and get rid of wrinkles. This formula is a great alternative to the many expensive anti-wrinkle formulas sold in stores. The honey will keep your skin glowing while the lemon juice breaks down wrinkles and scarring. The witch hazel or vodka will tighten your pores and eliminate bacteria and dead skin. Together, this solution produces bright, youthful skin!

Ingredients:

-2 teaspoons honey (raw is best)

-2 tablespoons witch hazel (or vodka)

-1 tablespoon lemon juice

Procedure:

-Mix ingredients

-Store in a glass jar and let sit for 3 days

-Apply morning and night

Lemon Astringent for Oily Skin

This astringent works wonders for those with oily skin, though it may be used by any skin type. The lemon juice and witch hazel work to rid the pores of bacteria, dead skin and excess oil. The result is minimized pores and a healthy, acne-free glow.

Ingredients:
-1/4 cup lemon juice
-1/2 cup witch hazel

Procedure:
-Mix ingredients
-Apply to the face with a cotton ball after regular cleansing

Lemon Feet and Hand Scrub and Skin
Softener

This softener will work wonders to
eliminate dry skin. You can use it
anywhere, but it works particularly well
on rough elbows, knees, feet and hands.

Ingredients:

-1/3 cup fine sea salt

-1/3 cup lemon juice

-1/3 cup olive oil

Procedure:

-Mix ingredients

-Massage into skin

-Rinse with warm water

-Apply moisturizer

Lemon Foot Soak

This lemon and cinnamon foot soak is a treat for tired, sore or dry feet. It's also simply relaxing. Try this soak once a week to keep your feet happy or whenever you need some time to yourself.

Ingredients:

-1/4 cup milk

-1 cup lemon juice

-2 tablespoons olive oil

-1/4 teaspoon cinnamon powder

Procedure:

-Mix ingredients into a warm tub of water

-Soak your feet for desired amount of time

-Rinse and moisturize

Relaxing and Rejuvenating Lemon Bath Soak

This citrusy formula makes a great bath soak. The scent of lemons will relax your stress away while the sea salt, milk and essential oils work to soften and rejuvenate your skin. Use this formula as often as you like for a simple, yet soothing treat.

Ingredients:

-1 cup powdered milk

-2 lemons

-3 cups sea salt (you can substitute rock salt or Kosher salt)

-lemon essential oil (for more fragrance, add any additional oils as you wish)

Procedure:

-Cut lemons into thin slices and place in a bowl

-Mix your essential oil and 1 teaspoon of
 salt into the bowl

-Mix powdered milk and remaining salt in
 another bowl

-Combine the contents of the two bowls
 and mix well

-Draw a warm bath, add your citrus mix
 and enjoy!

Lemon Nail Strengthener

If you have dry, weak, cracked, chipped or discolored nails, this simple solution can help. Olive oil will strengthen and moisturize your nails. Lemon juice will clean and brighten the nails, contributing to a healthy appearance. Use daily for the best results.

Ingredients:

-1 tablespoon lemon juice

-3 tablespoons olive oil

Procedure:

-Combine lemon juice and olive oil

-Microwave the mixture until warm (about 15 seconds)

-Stir to thoroughly combine ingredients

-Apply mixture to nails and cuticles (you may wish to use a cotton swab)

-Repeat each day

Lemon Dandruff Cure

Lemon is a natural antibacterial. It also works as an astringent and itch-reliever. Often, dandruff is caused by bacteria or excessive oils in the scalp. Using lemon is one of the cheapest, simplest and most effective ways to get rid of dandruff. With daily use, this formula will not only cure your dandruff problem, but will also give your hair a nice shine.

Ingredients:
-Lemon
-Water

Procedure:
-Squeeze the juice from a lemon into a glass of water
-Use this as your last rinse when cleaning your hair

Lemon Rinse for Shiny Hair

This simple formula will make your hair look shiny and healthy. If your hair isn't dry, you can use this solution everyday or whenever you want a little extra shine.

Ingredients:

-1 cup of water

-1 teaspoon lemon juice

Procedure:

-Mix ingredients

-Wash hair as normal

-Pour mixture over wet hair and massage in

-After a few minutes, rinse with cool water

How to Use Lemons for House and Laundry Cleaning

Contrary to what the cleaning product isle at your local grocery store may lead you to believe, you really only need a few basic ingredients to effectively clean your kitchen, bathroom and home. Often, common household cleaning products contain toxic chemicals and substances that can be harmful to the environment, you and your family. You can avoid using these dangerous and expensive products by making your own out of natural ingredients like lemons. For most cleaning jobs, you can make your own solutions using natural, safe, chemical-free components.

Window Cleaner
This vinegar and lemon juice mixture will cut through grease, fingerprints and tough stains to help you achieve a clean, sparkling window.

Ingredients:
-2 tablespoons lemon juice (without seeds)
-2 cups water
-Vinegar

Procedure:
-Mix the lemon juice and water in a spray bottle
-Fill the remainder of the bottle with vinegar

- -Shake to mix ingredients and use as desired

All-Purpose Disinfectant and Cleaning Spray

Creating your own homemade, all-natural, all-purpose disinfectant is easy! If you can, use a glass bottle as the acids in lemon can break down plastics. The vinegar and lemon juice in this cleanser have powerful germ-killing properties. You can use this refreshing, bacteria-killing spray in the kitchen, bathroom or any other area prone to mess and bacteria.

Ingredients:
-2 cups hot water

-1/2 cup white vinegar

-10-20 drops of lemon juice or essential lemon oil

-Glass spray bottle

Procedure:
-Mix ingredients into spray bottle

-To disinfect and clean surfaces, spray
  solution

-Let sit for 5 to 15 minutes

-Wipe clean

Wood Furniture Cleaner

Pledge is famous for its lemony wood cleaner. Instead of paying for that delicious-smelling clean, make your own wood furniture polish. This simple solution will clean wood and leave a nice shine.

Ingredients:

-1 cup olive oil

-1/2 cup lemon juice

-2 soft cloths

Procedure:

-Combine olive oil and lemon juice

-Use a soft cloth to apply to furniture and another to wipe it away

How to Unclog a Drain

Use this formula to unclog pipes and drains. The lemon juice will react with the baking soda, forming foam that will expand through the drain and pipe. The acidic juice and cleansing baking soda will work to dissolve the clog. For really tough clogs, you may want to repeat this process to make sure you get the entire gunk out.

Ingredients:
-Baking soda
-8 ounces lemon juice
-Boiling water

Procedure:
-Pour half a box of baking soda down the drain
-Pour in 8 ounces of lemon juice
-Leave for 30 minutes to an hour
-Pour hot or boiling water down the drain to sweep away clog

Gentle, Natural Hand Sanitizer

During cold and flu season, it's important to keep germs and bacteria from spreading around. But, many people are hesitant to lather on antibacterial gels-and for good reasons! Most gels contain alcohol and other chemicals that dry out the skin. They also often contain Triclosan, which can contribute to the creation of antibiotic-resistant superbugs. Keep yourself and your family healthy by mixing up your own batch of safe and natural hand sanitizer using essential oil.

Ingredients:
-4 oz glass spray bottle

-2 teaspoons aloe vera

-30 drops lemon essential oil

-10 drops vitamin E oil (optional hand moisturizer)

Procedure:

-Mix ingredients into spray bottle

-Fill the remainder of the bottle with
 water

-Shake and use as needed

Insect Repellant

This summer, avoid harmful pesticides by making a natural insect repellant.

Ingredients:
-Rosemary leaves

-1 Lemon

-Water

-Spray bottle

-Bowl

-Funnel

-Mesh strainer

Procedure:
-Cut and mash rosemary leaves into small pieces

-Cut lemon into thin slices

-Place lemon slices in bowl and sprinkle the rosemary on top

-Pour boiling water into the bowl and allow it to sit until cool

-Strain out the lemon slices and rosemary

-Use a funnel to pour remaining liquid
into a spray bottle

-To repel bugs, spray freely on skin and
clothing

Metal Cleaner

The acid content of lemons makes them
extremely useful in removing grease,
rust and stains from metals. Use this
formula to clean and polish copper,
bronze and brass (only real brass, don't
use on brass plated objects, lemon can
damage this material.

Ingredients:
Baking soda

Lemon juice

Procedure:
Combine baking soda and lemon juice
into a thick paste
If the solution is runny, add more

baking soda

Apply solution to metal with a soft cloth

and rub clean and rinse

Microwave Cleaner

If you don't clean it often, a microwave can build up grime and splatter stains that are difficult to get off. Luckily, lemon juice can help. Using this process, steam from a lemon juice and water mixture condenses on the walls, top and bottom of the inside of the microwave and acts on the grease and grime, allowing for easy clean-up. The more lemon juice condenses on the grime, the better it will dissolve and create the easiest microwave cleaning method possible.

Ingredients:
-1 lemon
-1 1/4 cups water
-Microwavable container

Procedure:

-Pour the water into your container

-Cut the lemon in half and add it to the
water

-Microwave the mixture for 5 to 10
minutes uncovered on maximum heat

-Remove container and wipe microwave
clean

Refrigerator Deodorizer

Lemon is a natural deodorizer. As such, it can be used as a safe, effective way to rid your refrigerator of unpleasant, lingering smells. For continuous deodorizing and freshening effects, put a new lemon in about once a week or when you start noticing lessening effects.

Ingredients:

-1 lemon

-Sock (optional)

Procedure:

-Cut up a lemon and place it in the refrigerator

-If you wish, you can put the cut up lemon in a sock

-Change the lemon every week or two

Plastic Storage Container Cleaner

Food containers sometimes accumulate food buildup, lingering smells and stains. Get rid of all of these problems without harsh chemicals by cleaning your containers with lemons.

Ingredients:

-Lemon or lemon juice

-Cloth

Procedure:

-Wipe lemon juice on containers

-Let sit for an hour or two before rinsing clean

Garbage Disposal Cleaner and Deodorizer

Get rid of a nasty garbage disposal smell using lemons. The peel will clean the disposal blades and the citrus will eliminate odors.

Ingredients:
-Lemon peel

Procedure:
-Place several pieces of a lemon peel in the disposal
-Turn on the faucet and disposal until clear

Vacuum Cleaner Deodorizer

Rid your vacuum cleaner of stale and unpleasant odors using lemon essential oil.

Ingredients:

-Lemon oil

-Paper towel or tissue

Procedure:

-Put several drops of lemon oil onto your paper towel or tissue

-Place the tissue in the collection bin or bag of the vacuum cleaner

-As you vacuum, the scent will disperse throughout the machine

Carpet Deodorizer

Baking soda and essential oils can be used to make a carpet deodorizer. If you so choose, you can replace the lavender oil with any other kind of essential oil to fit your preferences. The lavender may also be eliminated from this recipe. However, you may wish to include it or another oil to add a more pleasant scent. Don't add too much lemon oil. It is usually yellow and may stain the carpet if too much is used. If you have time to prepare the deodorizer the day before using it, do so. Letting the mixture sit overnight will allow the oils to better diffuse into the baking soda.

Ingredients:
-16 oz box of baking soda
-10 drops lemon essential oil

-20 drops lavender oil (may substitute or
  eliminate)

Procedure:
-Mix ingredients together
-Sprinkle mixture evenly over carpet (use
  a clean spice jar to make sprinkling
  easy)
-Leave the deodorizer for 10 to 40
  minutes
-Vacuum deodorizer away

Fragrance

Lemons have such a pleasant, refreshing smell. Simply catching the scent of a fresh lemon can give you a boost of energy and happiness. To keep your home smelling fresh and clean, use lemons as a natural fragrance. You can also add other ingredients for a bolder smell or mix them into a bottle for a fragrance spray.

Ingredients:

-1-3 lemons

-Mint, vanilla extract, rosemary or any other pleasant-smelling ingredients you like

-Water

Procedure:

-Combine ingredients in a pot

-Let simmer and allow the steam to
  spread pleasant fragrance throughout
  the house

Bleaching White Clothes with Lemon Juice

Instead of using bleach to get your white clothes clean, try lemon juice. Don't worry about over-bleaching, it's impossible to do with lemon juice. If you want, you can pour the juice/water solution in the washing machine with your clothes.

Ingredients:

-1/2 cup lemon juice

-1 gallon hot water

Procedure:

-Mix lemon juice and water

-Soak clothes for at least an hour

-Wash clothes as normal

Remove Rust from Clothes

You can also use lemon juice to remove rust stains from your clothes. Although some stains are tougher than others, soaking a stain in this solution for 15 to 30 minutes should be enough.

Ingredients:

-Lemon juice

-Cream of tartar

Procedure:

-Apply lemon juice to stain

-Sprinkle cream of tartar on top of stain and juice

-Rub the solution in and let sit 15-30 minutes or until stain is gone

-Wash clothes as normal

Laundry Deodorizer

You can use lemon juice to deodorize laundry and leave a fresh, pleasant scent.

Ingredients:

-10 drops lemon juice

Procedure:

-Add lemon juice to detergent

Lemon Cooking Recipes

Lemonade Recipes
Simply Sweet Lemonade

This delicious lemonade is sweet and satisfying. The following recipe makes about 10 8 oz servings. You can easily make a smaller or larger batch by adjusting the amounts of each ingredient in the proper ratio.

Ingredients:

-8 cups water

-1 1/2 cups lemon juice

-1 3/4 cups sugar

Procedure:

-Boil and stir the sugar and 1 cup of water together until sugar dissolves and let cool

-Cover and refrigerate the sugar water until cold

-Stir together the cold sugar water, lemon juice (with no seeds) and remaining water

-Enjoy!

Pink Lemonade

This pink lemonade recipe is quick and easy. For a creative serving, use a clear pitcher and garnish your lemonade with mint leaves and fresh fruit like lemon or orange wedges.

Ingredients:
-9 cups water

-2 cups sugar

-2 cups lemon juice (without seeds)

-1 cup cranberry juice

Procedure:
-Combine ingredients

-Stir to dissolve sugar

-Serve chilled or over ice

Healthy Vegetable Lemonade

This healthy lemonade recipe requires a juicer. It's packed with vitamins and nutrients and provides a fresh, satisfying alternative to traditional lemonade recipes.

Ingredients:

-1/2 inch piece of ginger

-1 head of lettuce

-4 kale leaves

-1 lemon

-2 apples

Procedure:

-Cut apples and lemons in half

-Juice all ingredients

-Enjoy!

Sparkling Lemonade Iced Tea

This green tea lemonade is refreshingly fizzy. The lime, seltzer water and green tea add some zing to the traditional flavor.

Ingredients:

-3 tablespoons sugar

-2 cups cool seltzer water

-2 cups hot water

-3 bags green tea

-2 teaspoons lemon juice without seeds

-1 sliced lime

Procedure:

-Place tea bags in hot water and let steep for 5 minutes

-Remove tea bags

-Stir in sugar until dissolved

-Chill the tea and sugar mixture

-Once cooled, add the seltzer and lemon
  juice

-Add lime slices for a fancy presentation
  and enjoy

Lemon Iced Tea

This drink combines two refreshing favorites- lemonade and iced tea! Add citrus slices for even more flavor and color!

Ingredients:
-2 large tea bags (any flavor you like)

-3 cups water

-1/2 cup sugar

-1- 1 1/2 cups lemon juice

-4 cups cold water

-1 oz (about 1 loose cup) mint leaves

Procedure:
-Boil 3 cups water

-Remove from heat

-Add tea bags and mint leaves. Steep for
  10 minutes

-Remove tea bags and mint

-Stir in sugar until dissolved

-Add cold water and lemon juice

-Serve chilled or over ice

Vegan Recipes

Lemon Vegan Stir-Fry

This delicious vegetarian, vegan stir fry has a light lemony taste.

Ingredients:

-1 sliced onion

-1 cup cooked or canned chickpeas

-Sea salt

-2 tablespoons extra virgin olive oil

-2 chopped zucchini

-8 oz firm, cubed tofu

-1 cup chopped kale

-Juice and zest of 1/2 lemon

Procedure:

-Heat 1 tablespoon olive oil in a skillet over medium-high heat

-Stir in onion, chickpeas and a big pinch of salt

-Sauté until chickpeas look golden and
  crusty

-Stir in the tofu and let cook for 1-2
  minutes

-Add kale and cook for 1 minute

-Empty the skillet onto a plate

-Heat the remaining olive oil

-Add zucchini to oil and sauté 2-3
  minutes

-Add the food from the plate back to the
  skillet and turn off heat

-Stir in lemon juice and zest

-Serve

Lemon Grilled Tofu

This recipe makes golden, flavorful tofu with achiote. You can serve it over a salad, pasta or any way you like!

Ingredients:
-1/4 teaspoon cayenne pepper

-2 pinches of salt

-2 tablespoons achiote powder

-3 peeled garlic cloves

-1 tablespoon brown sugar or raw cane sugar

-1/3 cup lemon juice (without seeds or pulp)

-12 oz tofu cut into 4 pieces

Procedure:
-Whisk sugar, achiote powder and cayenne pepper together

-Mince garlic and salt into a paste

-Whisk garlic paste, lemon juice and
  achiote mixture until combined
-Place tofu in an 8x8 baking dish
-Pour in marinade and cover tofu on all
  sides
-Place tofu in the refrigerator for a
  minimum of one hour (you can flip the
  tofu half way to marinade both sides
  evenly)
-Grill the tofu over medium heat, using
  the extra achiote marinade
-When both sides of tofu are golden with
  grill marks, remove and serve

Mexican Lemon Soup

This recipe makes four one cup servings of a healthy, protein-packed soup. It works best with Meyer lemon juice because of its milder lemon flavor.

Ingredients:

-4 whole cloves

-1 onion cut into quarters

-4 cups chicken broth

-2 seeded and quartered jalapeno peppers

-3 tablespoons grated lemon zest

-8 crushed and peeled cloves garlic

-1/2 teaspoon cumin seeds

-1 4 inch cinnamon stick

-3 tablespoons lemon juice

-1 lb peeled and deveined raw shrimp

-1/2 teaspoon salt

-1/2 cup fresh chopped cilantro

-1/4 teaspoon hot sauce (optional)

Procedure:

-Heat broth, garlic, zest, onion, jalapenos, cinnamon stick, cumin seeds and cloves in a large saucepan until simmering

-Reduce heat, cover and simmer for 20 minutes

-Strain out solids and discard

-Bring broth back to a simmer

-Add lemon juice, shrimp, salt and hot sauce

-After about 3 minutes, when shrimp are firm, turn off heat

-Stir in cilantro and serve

Garlic and Lemon Spaghetti

This garlic and lemon spaghetti has a sour, bitter and spicy flavor. The recipe makes four main course servings or about 8 servings if used as a side dish.

Ingredients:
-1 lb spaghetti

-Zest of two lemons

-1/2 cup extra virgin olive oil

-4 minced garlic cloves

-3/4 teaspoon dried hot red pepper flakes

-3 tablespoons lemon juice

-1/2 cup fresh parsley

-1 1/2 teaspoons salt

-1/2 teaspoon black pepper

Procedure:
-Cook pasta in boiling salt water

-Cook garlic and pepper flakes in oil over medium heat for 5 minutes or until garlic is golden

-Stir in zest, juice, salt, pepper and 1/2 cup water

-Bring ingredients to a simmer

-Then, add everything together and serve

Mashed Potatoes with Lemon Zest

The lemon zest in this recipe gives the mashed potatoes a bright, tangy flavor. This vegan recipe is a much healthier version of traditional mashed potatoes.

Ingredients:

-1 teaspoon salt

-4 medium potatoes

-Zest of 1 lemon

-1/2 teaspoon black pepper

-2 mashed garlic cloves

-3/4 cup extra virgin olive oil

-3/4 tablespoon thyme leaves

Procedure:

-Wash the lemon to remove pesticides

-Grate the zest and set aside

-Peel and wash potatoes

-Cut potatoes into 1/2 inch slices and put
  into a deep pan

-Add water until it is almost covering the
  potatoes

-Add salt, boil, cover and simmer for 15-
  20 minutes

-Gradually add the oil while mashing the
  potatoes

-Prior to serving, mix in garlic, lemon
  zest, thyme and pepper

Curd Recipes
Basic Lemon Curd

This recipe makes about 1 cup of delicious lemon curd.

Ingredients:

-1/4 cup lemon juice

-Zest of 1/2 lemon

-6 tablespoons sugar

-3 egg yolks

-4 tablespoons butter cut into pieces

Procedure:

-Whisk lemon zest, juice, yolks and sugar in a saucepan

-Put on medium heat and stir constantly

-Cook for about 5 minutes or until mixture is thick enough to coat stirring utensil

-Remove from heat

-Add butter, stirring until smooth

-Put curd in a bowl and cover directly
  with plastic wrap
-Let chill for an hour and serve when
  desired

Easy Lemon Curd

This is a simple recipe for a tasty lemon curd you can make in the microwave in just minutes!

Ingredients:

-1 cup sugar

-2 eggs

-1 cup lemon juice (freshly squeezed from 2-4 lemons without the seeds and pulp is best)

-1/2 cup melted butter

Procedure:

-Combine all ingredients in a large microwavable bowl (use an extra large bowl to prevent bubbling over)

-Microwave for 5 to 10 minutes in 1 minute increments stirring between each minute

-When curd is thick enough to coat the
 back of a spoon, it's done
-Refrigerate until firm or ready to eat

Low-Fat Lemon Curd

This light version of lemon curd is so flavorful, you won't even be able to tell it's healthy. It has a more intense flavor than traditional curd and will leave you pleasantly satisfied.

Ingredients:

-Zest from 1 lemon

-1 cup lemon juice

-2 eggs

-13 tablespoons castor sugar

-1 tablespoon cornstarch

-1 tablespoon butter

Procedure:

-Mix everything except the butter in a blender

-Pour into a pan with butter

-Cook at low heat, constantly stirring until thickened

-Cool and enjoy!

Holiday Spice Lemon Curd

This curd is perfect for Thanksgiving and Christmas get-togethers or holiday parties. A few extra ingredients add some spice to the classic lemony flavor.

Ingredients:

-2 eggs

-Zest of two lemons

-4 tablespoons butter

-3/4 cup sugar

-1/2 cup lemon juice (freshly squeezed without the seeds)

-1 cinnamon stick

-3 whole cloves

Procedure:

-Whisk juice, zest, cinnamon, cloves, butter and sugar in a saucepan over low heat until sugar dissolves and butter melts

-Add eggs, keep whisking

-Cook until thickened (about 10 minutes)

-Strain through a colander

-Refrigerate until chilled then enjoy!

Cookie Recipes
Basic Lemon Cookie

This recipe uses a cake mix for a fast, easy, scrumptious treat.

Ingredients:
-2 eggs

-3 teaspoons lemon juice

-1/3 cup vegetable oil

-1 lemon cake mix

-1/3 cup confectioner's sugar

Procedure:
-Preheat oven to 375 degrees F

-Mix eggs, oil, lemon juice and cake mix

-Drop small balls of dough into confectioner's sugar and roll around to coat

-Place on a cookie sheet and bake for 5 to 10 minutes

Lemon Tea Cookies

These cookies will be a hit with your family, friends or party guests. They're perfect for serving with tea.

Ingredients:

-2 cups flour

-1 1/2 teaspoons lemon zest

-4 sticks and 1/6 cup of room temperature butter

-2 2/3 cups powdered confectioner's sugar

-1/4 cup lemon juice (freshly squeezed is best)

-1/2 teaspoon vanilla extract

-1 1/2 cups cornstarch

Cookie Procedure:

-Preheat oven to 350 degrees F

-Beat 4 sticks of butter until creamy

-Mix in 2/3 cup powdered sugar until
  fluffy

-Beat in vanilla extract and 1 teaspoon
  lemon zest

-Add cornstarch and flour and mix well

-Roll dough into balls or use a cookie
  scoop

-Place balls of dough on cookie tray

-Bake 15 minutes

Icing Procedure:

-Combine 1/4 cup lemon juice, 1/6 cup
  butter, 2 cups powdered sugar and 1/2
  teaspoon lemon zest

-If the icing is too thick, add more lemon
  juice

Soft and Chewy Lemon Cookies

These sweet and tangy cookies have the perfect balance of texture. For even more lemony goodness, make a glaze to drizzle on top using 2 tablespoons of lemon juice and a cup of powdered sugar.

Ingredients:
-1 egg

-1 egg yolk

-1 tablespoon cornstarch

-1/2 teaspoon salt

-2 cups and 2 tablespoons flour

-1 1/4 cups sugar

-1/2 teaspoon baking soda

-3/4 cup softened butter

-2 tablespoons fresh lemon juice

-Zest of 2 lemons

-1 1/2 teaspoon vanilla extract

Procedure:

-Preheat oven to 350 degrees F

-Whisk flour, baking soda, cornstarch and salt together

-In separate bowl, mix butter, lemon zest and sugar together on medium-high speed for about 3 minutes

-Mixture should be fluffy

-Mix in egg, egg yolk, vanilla extract and lemon juice

-Add dry ingredients slowly, mixing until combined

-Form dough into balls and drop onto cookie sheets

-Bake 8 to 12 minutes

Lemon Sugar Cookie

These delectable, chewy sugar cookies have a light lemony flavor that will have you addicted!

Ingredients:

-2 1/4 cups flour

-1 teaspoon baking powder

-1/2 teaspoon baking soda

-1 egg

-1 tablespoon milk

-Zest from 1 lemon

-2 teaspoons lemon juice

-1/3 cup vegetable oil

-1/2 teaspoon salt

-1 teaspoon vanilla extract

-2 oz softened cream cheese

-2 cups sugar

-6 tablespoons melted butter

Procedure:

-Preheat the oven to 350 degrees F

-Whisk flour, baking soda, baking powder
  and salt together

-In a separate bowl combine cream
  cheese, 1 1/2 cups sugar and lemon zest

-Whisk in butter, milk, lemon juice, oil
  and egg

-Once soft dough forms, roll it into balls

-Roll the balls of dough in remaining
  sugar

-Place dough on cookie sheets and lightly
  flatten with the bottom of a glass cup

-Sprinkle some of the remaining sugar on
  top of the cookies

-Bake 10 to 14 minutes

Dessert Recipes
Lemon Tart

This simple lemon tart is delicious and easy to make.

Ingredients:

-2 eggs

-1/4 cup and 3 tablespoons confectioner's sugar

-1 cup sugar

-1 cup and 2 tablespoons flour

-2 tablespoons lemon zest

-1/2 cup softened butter

-1/4 teaspoon salt

-4 tablespoons lemon juice

Procedure:

-Heat oven to 350 degrees F

-Mix 1/4 cup confectioner's sugar and butter until smooth

-Mix in 1 cup flour

-Press dough into an 8x8 inch greased baking pan

-Poke dough several times to prevent a
 puffy crust

-Bake 10 to 15 minutes

-Whisk eggs and 1 cup sugar

-Add 3 tablespoons flour, zest, lemon
 juice and salt

-Pour this mixture on top of the baked
 crust

-Bake 20 to 25 minutes

-Once cool, top with 3 tablespoons
 confectioner's sugar

Easy Lemon Pudding
This tangy pudding is light and delectable. A treat for your tastebuds!

Ingredients:
-1/4 cup cornstarch

-3 egg yolks

-2 tablespoons soft butter

-2 1/2 cups milk

-3/4 cup white sugar

-2 tablespoons lemon zest

-1/2 cup lemon juice

-1/16 teaspoon salt

Procedure:
-Whisk cornstarch, sugar and milk
  together in a saucepan until smooth
-Lightly beat the egg yolks and add them
  to the saucepan
-Add salt and lemon zest
-Cook over medium heat

-Stir frequently until thickened

-Remove from heat and stir in butter and
 lemon juice

-Let cool

-Refrigerate and serve when chilled

Lemon Ice Cream

This recipe makes smooth and creamy lemon ice cream.

Ingredients:

-1 cup milk (whole milk works best)

-6 egg yolks

-4 teaspoons lemon zest

-1 1/2 cups heavy cream

-3/4 cup and 2 tablespoons sugar

-2/3 cup lemon juice

-Dash of salt

Procedure:

-Boil (and stir) cream, sugar, lemon zest, salt and milk until sugar dissolves

-Whisk egg yolks in a bowl

-Whisk cream mixture in with the eggs

-Return to saucepan and cook over low heat 3 to 5 minutes or until thickened, stirring constantly

-Once thick and 180 degrees F, add lemon
 juice

-Stir occasionally while letting cool to
 room temperature

-Chill then freeze in ice cream maker

Cake Recipes
Quick and Easy Lemon Cake
This cake is simple and satisfying with a
light lemon flavor.

Ingredients:

-1 cup sugar

-2 teaspoons lemon zest

-3/4 cup milk

-1/2 teaspoon salt

-1 egg

-1 1/2 teaspoons baking powder

-1 1/4 cups flour

-1 teaspoon lemon juice

-1/4 cup melted margarine or butter

Procedure:

-Preheat oven to 350 degrees F

-Mix sugar, baking powder, salt and flour in an 8x8 inch baking pan

-Mix lemon zest and egg together with fork

-Pour into pan with margarine

-Add milk and mix well

-Bake 30 to 35 minutes

-Cool and add icing and lemon zest on top

Lemon Sponge Cake

This lemon sponge cake is moist and savory.

Ingredients:

-Zest from 1 lemon

-3/4 cup butter

-3/4 cup flour

-3/4 cup sugar

-3 eggs

-3 tablespoons lemon juice

-3/4 teaspoon baking powder

-Dash of salt

Procedure:

-Beat butter and sugar until fluffy

-Add eggs

-Gently fold in lemon zest, juice, salt, baking powder and flour

-Bake for about 30 minutes at 350 degrees F

Lemon Pound Cake

This cake is so versatile. Enjoy it by itself, with fruit or with your favorite ice cream.

Ingredients:

-1 cups white sugar

-1/2 cup milk

-2 eggs

-1 tablespoon lemon juice

-1 1/2 cups self-rising flour

-1 stick of melted butter

Procedure:

-Mix butter and 1 cup sugar

-Beat eggs

-Add eggs and 1 tablespoon lemon juice to the butter and sugar mixture

-Mix in flour and milk

-Bake for 1 hour at 325 degrees F

Lemon Detoxification

How Does the Lemon Detox Work?

The lemonade detox diet, also known as the master cleanse, gained popularity after Beyonce Knowles used it to lose 20 pounds. However, this diet has been around for over 50 years gaining many fans along the way.

Stanley Burroughs first recommended the cleanse to patients suffering from stomach ulcers. After 11 days, the first patient was healed. Doctors were amazed as several other patients tried the master cleanse and achieved the same healing within 10 days. They also experienced weight loss.

The master cleanse works based on the idea that to be healed from disease, the body must be cleansed of toxins.

It is recommended that the diet be followed for at least 10 days to get the full benefits of the program. However, users may still benefit from a shorter cleanse.

The cleanse works by flushing out the digestive system and giving it a break from the toxins we put into our bodies each day. So, it is important to strictly stick to the lemonade recipe and not add any other vitamins, food or drink. The vitamins and minerals in the maple syrup and lemons are enough for the body during the cleanse.

The lemonade diet has several benefits in addition to cleansing the system. It helps users gain clarity of mind and freedom from addiction. As a participant progresses through the cleanse, they will begin to overcome the pain of hunger and be empowered. After a cleanse, many people report a lessened desire to eat sweets and other certain foods. Some even choose to become vegetarian after experiencing the power of a cleanse.

Getting Started on a Detox Cleanse Diet

Before doing a cleanse, it is important to make sure you are ready both physically and mentally. Otherwise, failure is highly likely. You will get hungry and most likely experience at least one other side effect such as constipation, diarrhea, fatigue, dizziness or headache.

If you drink caffeine regularly, you should work on cutting back before starting a cleanse. If you suddenly stop giving your body the caffeine it is used to, there is a very high chance that you will experience withdrawal headaches and other side effects.

Some people prepare for a cleanse by eating a vegetarian diet in the days or weeks leading up to it. A vegetarian diet is easier on the body and will make the transition to a lemonade diet easier.

Let's Start

The diet involves drinking a sort of lemonade.

Lemonade Recipe

-10 oz. hot or cold water
-2 tablespoons genuine maple syrup
-2 tablespoons lemon or lime
-1/10 teaspoon cayenne pepper

Burroughs suggests drinking a minimum

of six to twelve 10 ounce glasses of the lemonade daily. This will provide 650 to 1300 calories and likely cause 2 or 3 pounds of weight loss each week.

He also says mint tea and plain water are allowed. In addition, laxatives must be taken each day to ensure that toxins are being eliminated from the body. A saltwater flush or herbal tea laxative is suggested.

During the first few days of a cleanse, you will experience the most side effects. Headache, digestive symptoms and fatigue are the most common. For this reason, it is recommended that you begin a cleanse on the weekend or during a time when you are free from obligations like work. This will give you time to let your body adjust.

After the first few days, sticking to a cleanse usually becomes easier. Hunger pangs will subside and you should feel energized. Many cleanse participants report entering a state of bliss and tranquility, possibly as a result of reduced toxicity.

Getting Out of Detox Diet

After the 10 days, or however long you choose to participate in a cleanse, it is important to properly introduce food to the body. It is recommended that the first day start with only orange juice or other juices. The second day, drink orange juice in the morning and try light vegetable soups or broth for lunch and dinner. The third day, eat fruits, vegetables and a few rye crackers. On the fourth day, you may return to your regular diet with caution. You should eat slowly and in small amounts until you are confident that your system is ready to handle the food.

Possible Dangers of Doing a Cleanse

Participating in a cleanse can be hard on the body. So, it is not recommended for everyone. In general it is safe for everyone but it is recommended that every participant should consult his/her family doctor before starting and if any problem occurs during the program follow the advice of your doctor. And specially –

• If you have any medical conditions, consult your doctor before beginning any kind of cleanse or diet.

• If you are underweight, do not do a cleanse. Additional weight lost during a cleanse could be dangerous. The master cleanse involves a calorie deficit, so weight will be lost. If you do not have excess fat, your body will turn to muscle, even your heart muscle, as a source of energy. This can be extremely dangerous.

• Those on immunosuppressive drugs

or anyone who has had an organ transplant may not participate in a cleanse. Because the master cleanse stimulates the immune system, the effects of these types of drugs will be inhibited and the body will reject the organ.

Final Words

I hope you must have not only enjoyed this book but also tried few recipes for your cooking, cleaning, skin and hair care. If you want to let others know about your experience, please post your valuable and constructive reviews. Your feedback matters and it really does make a difference.

I would greatly appreciate your comment because your review is going to help me improve and update my work. If you found any error or anything you suggest to change or add in this, do let me know at ypamesh@gmail.com and I promise a quick personal response.

Your review is going to make a true experience for other readers and help them make their buying decision easier. If you'd like to leave a review then all you need to do is go to review section of book and click on "Write a customer review".

Also by ADISH Books are the following books –

Essential Oils Beauty Secrets: Make Beauty

Products at Home for Skin Care, Hair Care, Lip Care, Nail Care and Body Massage for Glowing, Radiant Skin and Shiny Hairs

Scrubs and Masks: 50 Simple Natural Homemade Recipes for Glowing Radiant and Younger Skin by Exfoliation, Moisturizing and Nourishing Facial Masks for All Skin Types

Coconut Oil: Recipes for Skin Care, Hair Care, Healthy Smoothies, Muffins, Soup, Salad, Chicken and Desserts

Juicing Magic: 50+ Recipes for Detoxification, Weight Loss, Healthy Smooth Skin, Diabetes, Gain Energy and De-Stress

Made in the USA
Middletown, DE
10 October 2014